DATE OF BIRTH

ABOUT THE LEXI RUDNITSKY FIRST BOOK PRIZE IN POETRY

The Lexi Rudnitsky First Book Prize in Poetry is a collaboration between Persea Books and The Lexi Rudnitsky Poetry Project. It sponsors the annual publication of a collection by a female-identifying poet who has yet to publish a full-length poetry book.

Lexi Rudnitsky (1972–2005) grew up outside of Boston. She studied at Brown University and Columbia University, where she wrote poetry and cultivated a profound relationship with a lineage of women poets that extends from Muriel Rukeyser to Heather McHugh. Her own poems exhibit both a playful love of language and a fierce conscience. Her writing appeared in *The Antioch Review, Columbia: A Journal of Literature and Art, The Nation, The New Yorker, The Paris Review, Pequod*, and *The Western Humanities Review*. In 2004, she won the Milton Kessler Memorial Prize for Poetry from *Harpur Palate*. Lexi died suddenly in 2005, just months after the birth of her first child and the acceptance for publication of her first book of poems, *A Doorless Knocking into Night* (Mid-List Press, 2006). The Lexi Rudnitsky First Book Prize in Poetry was founded to memorialize her and to promote the type of poet and poetry in which she so spiritedly believed.

PREVIOUS WINNERS OF THE LEXI RUDNITSKY FIRST BOOK PRIZE IN POETRY

2021 Anni Liu, *Border Vista*
2020 Sarah Matthes, *Town Crier*
2019 Sara Wainscott, *Insecurity System*
2018 Valencia Robin, *Ridiculous Light*
2017 Emily Van Kley, *The Cold and the Rust*
2016 Molly McCully Brown, *The Virginia State Colony for Epileptics and Feebleminded*
2015 Kimberly Grey, *The Opposite of Light*
2014 Susannah Nevison, *Teratology*
2013 Leslie Shinn, *Inside Spiders*
2012 Allison Seay, *To See the Queen*
2011 Laura Cronk, *Having Been an Accomplice*
2010 Cynthia Marie Hoffman, *Sightseer*
2009 Alexandra Teague, *Mortal Geography*
2008 Tara Bray, *Mistaken for Song*
2007 Anne Shaw, *Undertow*
2006 Alena Hairston, *The Logan Topographies*

DATE OF BIRTH
POEMS
SHAWN R. JONES

A KAREN & MICHAEL BRAZILLER BOOK
PERSEA BOOKS / NEW YORK

Persea Books, Inc.
90 Broad Street
New York, New York 10004

Library of Congress Control Number: 2023931037

Book design and composition by Rita Lascaro
Typeset in Baskerville
Manufactured in the United States of America.
Printed on acid-free paper.

This book is dedicated to The Great Eight,
who were not intimidated by the odds
and changed the trajectory of our family.

In memory of Elizabeth Jones (1926–1941),
of whom we do not speak,
but deserves to be remembered

ACKNOWLEDGMENTS

I am grateful to the editors of the following journals in which these poems, sometimes in different versions, first appeared:

Cider Press Review:
>   "1454 Gladys St."
>   "Dentist Appointment During the Pandemic"

Guesthouse:
>   "Hypoglycemia During the COVID-19 Crisis"

Langston Hughes Review:
>   "Listening to Donna Summer Reminds Me of My Father"
>   "One Reason She Keeps a Switchblade in Her Pocket"

New Ohio Review:
>   "On Our Way Back from the Protest"

Obsidian (48.1, pages 34–36):
>   "Dirty Little Secrets Are Just Another Set of Facts"
>   "Dog Fight in the Virginia Avenue Courts"

The Passengers:
>   "I Was Going to Name You Oni"
>   "After Our Pit Died on the Porch in My Husband's Arms"
>   "Spying on Uncle Hector"

Peregrine Journal:
>   "Finding Uncle's Dead Body"

Rattle:
>   "Soprano from the Junior Choir at the Protest"

River Heron Review:
>   "Admission of Guilt"

TriQuarterly:
>   "Today My Cousin Brenda Would Have Been 50"

Typehouse:
   "The Undertow"
   "To My Neighbor Who Had the *All Lives Matter* Sign on Her
      Lawn"
   "Eenie Meenie Miney Moe"
   "Afraid to Open This Letter from Inmate 17650-328"

I am also grateful to the following people who helped usher *Date of Birth* into the world:

Jeffrey H. Jones, for your full acceptance of me and every line I have ever written, giving every poem a home in your heart, and decades of love, support, and encouragement.

Jade R. Jones, for reading my work, encouraging me to apply to graduate school, being my unpaid personal assistant, reminding me to set boundaries, and cheering me on through every step of the process.

Grayson Morley, for celebrating every publication and sharing my work on social media.

Jeffrey C. Jones, for reading my work and being a light of hope, faith, and encouragement.

Julia Jones, for reading my work, encouraging me, and for editorial and formatting advice.

Rashonda Robinson, for hours of heartfelt discussions about Black womanhood and family history and for teaching me that "honesty doesn't require literal truth, and literal truth is no guarantee of honesty."

Rhonda C. Fitzgerald, for mothering me through the storms, holding me above the clouds, and carrying me over the rainbow.

My aunts, Princess and Linda Jones and Great Aunt Connie Green, for your transparency and research of our family's history.

Maude Jones, for telling me, "One day you are going to be famous in the literary world."

Rhonda I. Fitzgerald, for teaching me that even the darkest poems have something to offer and for reading my manuscript and telling me with all sincerity that you loved every poem.

Gregory Pardlo, my amazing thesis advisor, for listening, believing in my work, and teaching me to write fearlessly.

Patrick Rosal, for teaching me not to be afraid to walk in the wilderness of my own words and also for creating a safe space for me to speak and write without judgement.

Peter Murphy, for allowing me to grow as a writer in a non-competitive atmosphere and for years of friendship and mentorship.

David Wanczyk, for excellent editorial advice.

Rachel Ward-DiGiovanni, Tanya Cain, Frieda Halliday, Marah Blake, Marcia LeBeau, J.C. Todd, Paul Lisicky, Judith Lagana, Robin Farr, J.T. Barbarese, Arlene Edmonds, and Rick Weems, for your consistent support and encouragement.

Friends from No River Twice, *Langston Hughes Review*, Collingswood Book Festival, Rutgers-Camden MFA, and Winter Poetry and Prose Getaway.

Gabriel Fried, my editor, and the outstanding Persea staff for your support, expertise, and professionalism.

Tajh Rust, for a stunning cover!

God, for my life and another day to write.

CONTENTS

DATE OF BIRTH

Dirty Little Secrets Are Just Another Set of Facts

Grandmother tried to extract me from the womb
with a metal hanger one year before the bellhop shot
her in AC. Mom took acid. Ran around like a cartoon
before jumping off the jetty. Drowned at thirty.

Cops pulled a train on a white officer. Grandpop
was the only one arrested. *Oh, I wanted it,* she said, *but
the coon wasn't invited.* Dogs found dad in the backseat
of a junkyard jeep at fifty-five. Pushers called him *greedy.*

My children married white people. My aunt asked
where I went wrong. I said, *Maybe they are trying to stay
alive a few more generations.* I never judged her
for her crimes or the dismantled gun in the wall.

Brother put his son in a trash bag. Proof of mens rea,
the linchpin of the case spun from manslaughter to murder
in the first degree. Buried him in the same sand where our small
fingers had bustled under the boards to make castles.

Twenty-five years later, his trigger hands still shake, so how can I
incubate in this ivory house? Write myself free? I am blood bound.
I am a weapon: mom's dirty little secret, brown embryo born blue.
Twisted hanger reshaped. Strange words made from wire.

Jonathan Louis James Jr. Was a Poet

"That Johnnie was one pretty nigga who could rhyme."
—My dad's friend Sammy

It was three am. I had to pee. I wonder if I could have saved
him if I had gotten up to pee a few minutes sooner.

All night I had been running away from the image
of my father dying. It was my fifteenth birthday.

Twenty-four hours had not yet passed since I had run off, so
Mother called the Seashore Baptist Church at the end of our block.

We were not members, but we had been there two Easters in a row.
Pastor Stone and the deacons searched the city in the most likely

places I would hide. Pastor found me sleeping under the boardwalk
with a sandy bed and seaweed pillow. I refused to go back to my house.

I stayed with Pastor and his wife. They made me a peanut butter
sandwich at my request. Hired me to clean the church. Listened to me

talk about my father. Valued each story. Understood my dad was not
just a junkie who overdosed on the bathroom floor. My Dad had jazz

in his fingertips when he wrote my mother love letters from the county
jail. I found them a decade later. Unfolded the wrinkled papers.

Flattened the pages. Deciphered penciled text. Rebirthed his lines.
Wrote my lovers' names in the salutations. Left the body unchanged.

My daddy was a poet. His life, poetry. He improvised words
with authentic swag. "One pretty nigga" who made lyric out of city.

Seven

For my mother

Under a crippled limb tree, held by two slabs
of slanting wood, behind a single chained fence

hooked to rusty metal poles with jagged heads
and chipped green paint, in balding grass

and cold cracked-gray dirt, I fought green-eyed
Ella as the neighborhood kids cheered her on.

Then I saw my mother, slender and brown,
come out the screened door of our red brick apartment

with one hand on the hip of black slacks. I remember
her tight cheekbones, arched nostrils, charcoal

wavy hair, shadowing her right eye, falling over
a gray turtleneck shirt onto confident shoulders,

and that mole, standing on glossy lips, stoned
by anger as her dark eyes with horse lashes

dammed my tears and owned that moment
when her deep voice cheered me on.

Home Remedy 1968

Debris had fallen months
before my unwanted arrival
when grandmother gave
her unwed daughter
tar black pills to swallow
behind Tanqueray gin,
mixed turpentine and hot water
in a pea green bucket,
held mom's flannel gown
around her stretched waist,

and told her to crouch down
as close as she could get.

I Was Going to Name You Oni

Hand over hand I pulled
from womb that would not

let go all at once. I mourned ruby
chunks dangling over porcelain

before they dropped away from me.
I cradled ruddy nugget hands,

smeared cherry fingertips
with index finger and thumb,

wrote your would-be name on tile
with what was left of you.

Finding Uncle's Dead Body

The one who touched me
moved into 1454 before the sheriff

padlocked the door.
I'd gone to collect an apology.

I found him in the nursery
with his porn, gerbils in cages,

and Playmates taped over
a mural of Care Bears

sharing an umbrella
under a cloud of balloons.

His torso was twisted
across a twin mattress.

Blue of neck
alone in the cold

was not price enough.
He got off

cheap. I am still not okay

because I don't
know what to do

with myself
now that he is gone,

and I have no other target
for this hate,

but my own
incensed body.

Eloise Speaks

I prayed in the throat of my father's house.
He frowned with mushroom wilted lips,
eyeing gin and bottles of Percocet
on the nightstand as death groomed
his hair and spiders snuggled in towels
dampened by waste—waste that softened
sores on his bottom as he discharged his sin—
sin that whined through the mouths of saints
at his funeral, who said,

He did just want he wanted to do,

and everyone knew what that meant, but
they all nodded like it was okay,
and pews full of daughters and I
blamed ourselves
and still blame ourselves
for sibling offspring
long after Father has been lowered
into the ground.

And the church still said, *Amen,*
And the church still said, *Amen*
And the church
still said,
Amen

while babies ascended from backyard graves
and praise danced down center aisles,
clear arms and legs swinging
pale and silent,
slinging dirt across the red casket
as the elder choir sang,

Am . . . zing Grace, in white robes on black skin
below an old brass crucifix
that rattled like loose pipes in tight walls.

But I will never sing.
Nor will I say, *Amen,*
remembering the ruffle at nightfall,
the newborn baby crying, and daddy
walking away with bucket
and shovel in hand.

Spying on Uncle Hector

I often wondered if Uncle
bopped down our walk
like an ordinary man
before he came to our house.

I wondered if he had
a spikey tail that retracted
into his spine
like some creature wanting
to conceal its identity.

But I detected nothing
from where I hid
behind curtains

in the front window.
I watched him
cover his head
in the rain and drag
mud across the walk
that led to our door.

He hopped off his bike,
kicked down his kickstand,
and looked over his right shoulder
before he knocked.

Wiped his feet
on the braided mat. Shook off
his camouflage coat.

Hung it on the rack
in the corner
by the lamp and table.
Gripped the banister
with his knotted hand
on his way to your room.

Tied little brother
to an armchair in the hall.

Kissed you with his head
shrouded under your plaid skirt.

Gave you five pennies
to keep quiet.

One Reason She Keeps a
Switchblade in Her Pocket

The house key on a shoestring around her neck unlocks
the front door to Stanley Homes Village. Three boys are on
her back. They are in heat, but the chase is over. Paws
are on the edges of her shirt in the middle of the living
room where she played with her doll, Tamu, and watched
The Brady Bunch, *Good Times*, and *Bugs Bunny*. The rug burns
where she ate Apple Jacks, Fruit Loops, and Captain Crunch.

She is the only child. Has everything. Was taught to share, but they
demand "pussy." Even in fourth grade she knows what they ask
is taboo. They are in sixth. Learned pussy was something to be taken.
She learns it is something she will fight to keep. She scrambles across
the carpet to the kitchen floor. Pulls a knife from the drawer next
to the stove. Swings, cuts the air, slits one face. The boys haul ass.
Trip each other out the door. Cherry drips from the tip of the blade.

You Grow Up but Never Grow
Out of Your Nickname from AC

Tulu
short for Too Little
aka Tammy

Assa Bassa Bald Spot
aka Angela
had a patch of hair missing
on the back of her head

Wingwom
woke up with a ringworm on her cheek

Titty Meat
a chubby toddler
now seventy

Nose
named after her nose

Nose Jr.
Nose's little sister

Spaghetti Om
after a scar left from a burn
short for Spaghetti Arm

Tuna
aka Tina
didn't have hot water

Lady Bear
walked on her toes
tall with long hair

Low Booty
had a butt close to her knees

Baby Huey
after the huge cartoon duck

Big Daddy
shortest boy in high school

Black Rock
aka Ronald aka Ronnie
dark skin with a bald head

Bread
little girl with a big stomach

Buttaball
Bread's mom

Butt
aka Invisible Butt
his jeans sagged

Catfish
aka Ricky
had a hairy mole
next to his left nostril

Chunk
loved chocolate

Demon
aka Damon
stayed on suspension

Dirty Butt
only had one pair of pants

Doo Doo Brown
aka Derrick Brown

Donkey Kong
aka Donald Kelly

Dump
aka Danny Johnson
got thrown in the dumpster

Do Black
aka Donavan Blackman

Yak Yak
talked real fast

Tiger Lily
talked to herself

Hollywood
aka Sandra
played Dorothy in the school play

Pissy
wet the bed once

Milkman
didn't look like his mom or dad

Wayne Wayne Door Stain
aka Wayne

Ribbiedibs
aka Regina Harris

Lunchbox
aka Shawn Jones the Bag of Bones

Brother Johnnie Walker Blue

Stale beer, smoke, and sweat
ride the dancer's undulating waist

as wistful eyes chase her
wandering hips. On the counter,

Johnnie falls asleep with lips
the color of wet concrete

and a frothy grin that marinates
his chin for the barmaid's kiss.

On a leather stool, his son drinks
coke and smokes candy cigarettes

as he's schooled on being the man
who drones wordlessly in his sleep.

Dog Fight in the Virginia Avenue Courts

Kim, my older cousin
who knew how to start trouble,
pushed me out the door
to fight Sandra like a dog.

She put a stick on my shoulder
and dared Sandra
to knock my mother off the toilet.
The twig pirouetted behind my back
and landed on the remains of Ring Pops,
Gobstoppers, and Bottle Caps.

My shoulder, the slender branch,
the cold ground covered
with sharp edges from the Silver
Lounge, meant something.
We were poetic
before we read poems.

I jabbed Sandra's left cheek
just like I had jabbed her sister's
the week before. There was no escape.
I fought a different girl in the same
plot of dirt that used to grow daisies.

Surrounded by concrete borders,
crumpled packs of Virginia Slims,
and a ring of witnesses screaming,
made me feel like a champion.

Kim still brags about how
I *beat her ass* with an uppercut,
referring to Sandra
with the green eyes.

Sandra was golden. She knew how to fight
and had light skin—Queen of the Courts.
I couldn't let her have both titles

and watch the hood crown her
with candy, cigarettes,
and a confetti of broken glass.

I had to win.

1454 Gladys St.

The last home
I shared with my mother
and siblings
in Ventnor City was a sandstone
bungalow near the lagoon
beside the sewer plant
that inhaled the stench of summer,
dice, sweat, and booze.

I remember
phlegm in wine
glasses on our kitchen
counter, church bells
from St. Johns
on the corner,
and the foreclosure
sign on the front
door, marigold
on a wooden mouth
taped shut.

I had left long before,
escaping to a marriage
that was nowhere near
Gladys, and now I feel
some kind of way
I will always feel
coming back to this
home in memory
the way my family returned
themselves to salvage
what they could
when they could.

Nothing and
everything remained.

Mushrooms sprouted
from moist carpet.
Food in the fridge
was lined with mold.
Mice scrabbled
in drop ceilings.
Salt from the ocean
creeped and peeled
paint from plastered walls.

Somehow, they stayed.
There was nothing for me there,
and when I peeked
in the windows the night
before the boards went up,
everyone's ghost,
cushioned the backs
of wooden chairs.

Listening to Donna Summer Reminds Me of My Father

My dad sings "Last Dance" as he balances a joint
between his lips then chases it with a can of Natty Bo
while I build a house out of eight track tapes,

using forearms, elbows, and thighs to keep the house
from falling. *The Untouchables* flash white and black
silence from the Magnavox. Dad hands me more eight tracks.

The chunky cartridges with different color casings hold
prerecorded music of dad's favorite songs. I can still see blue
Temptations, pink Hendrix, and orange Mathis. Mom passes

small papers whiter than Sunday wafers. Dad rolls, pulls, and holds.
Blows shapes of dogs, cats, and dinos above my plastic town.
Laughs till he blows that image of his mother wilting, cancerous

limbs soft and brown. He was ten, but her immortal moans strum
through him. Notes corkscrewed like they belong there. A one man
band. Cries off key. I know he is thinking of her dying, and I regret

not dancing with him when he extends his outstretched hand.

Ghouls on Washington Street

1.

In Center City Camden,
row homes huddled together
on Washington Street. There were thirteen
brownstones, three stories high.
The middle nine had paying tenants.
The two on each end, squatters.

We were all neighbors, the boards
and the blinds. Shared the same spirits
wafting between walls after three am.
Recited the same prayers to vanquish
demons whose eyes glowed
like crimson fireflies till dawn.

2.

Esther told me to scrub my porch
down with water and bleach
because demons like dirt. I was too proud
to listen. She'd moved to Jersey
from Louisiana and roasted a whole pig
out back, blank stare and all.

I watched her stack three layers
of cinder block. Make a bed of coal.
Light a fire. Rest a grate on top.
Grill a hog for hours. Slap its scraps
on a plate. Season it with lizard sauce.
Of course, she believed in spirits.

3.

My son drew a *headless angel,* with crayon-
brown legs coming out the wall. Hung it
on the fridge with two magnets. Said it visits
him at night and walks backwards. *You're telling
stories,* I said. I thought he was delusional,
but I called Esther. Didn't tell her why.

She sat next to me on my step.
Placed a tiny bottle of olive oil
in my palm. Rolled my fingers
into a fist. Prayed for fifteen minutes.
Quoted James 4:7. Greased my forehead
Helped me anoint my home.

She got rid of Goosebumps, Gargoyles,
Nintendo, and The Wizard of Oz.
Prayed in every room. Rebuked demons.
Rubbed oil on every door, window, vent,
and headboard. Decluttered every corner.
Left gospel music playing on every floor.

4.

Before she lumbered home, she told me
to w*atch out for the mean one with no head.*
I thought of my son's drawing. Maybe he wasn't
delusional. I felt relieved, but less confident
in my disbelief. I never saw demons,
but after Esther's visit, I heard them

talking in voices low and guttural,
Lay him dead. Move over. Let us in.
I shoved clothes, soap, toothpaste
and deodorant in trash bags. Left holy
oil on the table in the vestibule with
instructions for whoever moved in after us.

That house made a believer out of me.

Admission of Guilt

Their first home was in the bowels of Camden.
I gave them birth. It gave them depth
for wherever their wooden legs would take them.

They would remember the shack
out back with no windows
men and women coming in and out

of its wounded orifices like rodents
foraging for food, sex, drugs.
They would remember the 75 pounds of cocaine

that fell from the sky and landed
on our freshly poured stoop.
It fell like snow, so I told them,

It is snow,
but keep your tongue
in your mouth.

They would remember the woman
running naked in front of my car with rain
shrunken hair and bloody beige breasts.

They would also remember
yellow buses carrying them a couple towns
over to an immaculate school

where they were not allowed
to color Jesus
or the angels brown.

Eenie Meenie Miney Moe

I eenie meenie miney moe around
the starfish-shaped collage of miniature feet
and stop at my grandson's, black with white laces.

I choose him, so he doesn't have to bury
his face in pretzeled arms or search
for friends who don't want to be found.

I choose him because the badge will
pursue him so many times,
he may become too tired to run.

I choose him, so he doesn't have to
plead for his life with the same deep dark eyes
that will see nightmares flash on the screen.

I choose him because he came in the world
knowing and unknowing one too many
lies about white Jesus and democracy.

I choose him because I am afraid
he will become one tear, fat with salt
as a blue faucet pushes him to the ground,

our plush drowning.

To My Neighbor Who Had the
All Lives Matter Sign on Her Lawn

When the cop spilled bullet-brown milk, the authorities
told the country not to cry over spilled milk.

The *All Lives Matter* sign danced across your lawn
with bare feet, a beer in one hand, toothpick

between pink lips, and shimmied with the neighbors
in your backyard while your daughter climbed

the aluminum siding of the house next door
where the black boy she loved smiled

from his window, holding the other end of a sheet
she had wrapped around her waist. Woman,

you were only one generation from brown.

A decade or two later you understood
when you saw a cop through the peep hole

of your suburban door. Your hand shook
as you turned the brass knob, and he told you

your very own grandson, *tainted* brown,
who you thought was safe cause he could pass

as an infant, had been shot. Something happened
during puberty that you did not expect, brown skin

and coils because he refused to cut his hair,
and like Kaepernick took a bow toward Africa.

But it was too late for you to go in reverse. Too late
to proclaim, *Black Lives Matter* when that guilty cop,

who pulled the trigger, dined at home with his family
while you cried at the grave of a brown child

you never imagined you could love.

Soprano from the Junior Choir at the Protest

Her larynx is raw from chanting.
Every diphthong, and syllable aflame.
Each vowel broken. She cannot sing,

We Shall Overcome. That was
her grandmother's song. And she
is not her grandmother.

So, forgive her for wanting
the police precinct destroyed.
Forgive her for cheering

as patrol cars scream between
flames. Forgive her for looting
the Smoke Shop in the alley

on James Street. Forgive her
for listening to Floyd cry,
Momma four hundred times

on her cell phone as she fills
a bong with kerosene.
Forgive her as she sticks a rag

in its petite mouth, turns
the soft pink cloth into wick,
and lights a kiss.

Forgive her as she becomes
the embodiment of rage—
hands, feet, and heart detached

mechanical movements,
unthinking. Forgive her.
Forgive her as she leans back,

steps forward, shifts her full
body weight, twists her torso,
drives her elbow forward,

and releases the bong—
a torched bird
with variegated wings.

On Our Way Back from the Protest

The officer approaches. Keith keeps both hands
on the steering wheel. Clicks his tongue

against his teeth six times—
a tune of feigned assurance.

The trooper walks back to his car.
Keith takes his hands off the wheel.

I am the first to speak. I ask if he thinks
the cop is going to give us a ticket?

The man who answers, *I don't know,*
is not my husband. He is not the man

who killed the wolf spider on the windowsill.
Not the man who grabbed a snake by its tail,

carried its body, wiggling to the ravine. Not the man
who beat down a thief twice his size in our home.

Not Keith who danced at the end of the protest
like it was a Sunday in New Orleans' Congo Square.

Or the man who arranged hydrangeas
tenderly, steadily beside his father's casket.

No. Tonight, he becomes Freddie,
Breonna, Botham, George.

Eyes the cop through the rearview mirror.
Puts both hands back on the steering wheel.

Drums the leather with his thumbs.

Divided We Fall

Death is dark with depth.
Bodies fall one
over the other

too weak to swim
against the current—
a twister of blue

and black bodies
spin to sludge,
to mush.

The old mother
with copper limbs
and nightlight in hand

swaddles and carries
her children in red,
white, and blue linen,

hushing them
till she can no longer
walk on water.

Hypoglycemia During the COVID-19 Crisis

She is on the stairs.
Hears two
sacks of potatoes
dropping. The sound,

body hitting tile.
The image, dark
rag doll drenched
between toilet and wall.

He is Black.
Too afraid
to go to the hospital.
Too afraid

to be denied
a ventilator.
Too afraid
to suffocate alone.

Remembering
Tuskegee,
she plays nurse.
Googles symptoms.

Takes his vitals
with her own hands.
Feeds him chocolate
from her palm.

Nothing's Different but the Color of the Sawdust

You know the girl my neighbor calls *Junkie*
because she's brown, even though she grew up

in town with my neighbor's son who has the same
disease after getting into some *mischief in Camden?*

I'm talking about Kelly with the acrylic fingernails
who scratches her arms and legs till they flake and fall

to the ground like sawdust. She's gone. Not to rehab.
To the state pen. Yet my neighbor's son's back

from camp for the fifth time. Cops keep locking Kelly up
six years for smack and petty theft while Brandon's

free. But my neighbor's forced to see
her own child relapse at home, leaving

blond sawdust in the shed, the garage, and Prius.
She tries to keep it hidden, uses

the sawdust to mulch. Lines the front of her house
with brick. Puts on lavender work gloves

with the cuffs flipped back. Lugs that load
in a wheelbarrow. Red-faced in a garden hat.

Dentist Appointment During the Pandemic

Masked staff behind plexiglass barriers.
No one in the waiting room.
Someone takes your temperature.
Leads you to another door.

The hygienist is suited up
to handle a hazard.
Gown, gloves, double mask:
all white, except
her teal booties.
She speaks, but you can't
hear what she's saying.

You are the contaminant
now. But you'll be on
your best behavior, as always.
No one needs to feel
threatened here.

When you're done, she'll call
for backup. And another attendant
who won't look over
will escort you out
as fast as possible.

It isn't much different
from how you have felt
your entire life.

Retreat

Amber must get away from her seven-figure
hell in the city. Blitz. The most popular hotel
in Monterey. Twenty-five stories facing the ocean.

A gift from her late brother who died of a stroke
earlier that summer. She thinks she's next.
Decides to take a trip to Pikes Peak.

Her tires crunch across the driveway of the mountain
chalet. She gets out of the Hummer. Pulls a blade
from her right boot. Slits the tires. Watches squirrels

scamper through piles of leaves, reminding her
that she hasn't played outside in a while.
In the middle of brown fern, cardinals bathe

in a cracked birdbath full of tree bits and green water.
She twitches, startled by a chipmunk running
through his drainpipe home with no mortgage.

She rips her clothes off and scurries naked on all fours
across swollen tree roots, dirt, and dead grass,
chasing behind a wild, crazy-eyed racoon.

Habit and Hips

no cup
soft eyes
clear with youth
almost mistook her
for sober

she has only been using
a short while
skin smooth like
suburban sheets

body not dilapidated
brick house junkie
no missing or broken windows

damned damsel
passing car
on husband's side

he tilts his pelvis
forward and lifts
pulls bill from jean pocket

calls, *Babe*!
I grow fangs
hate her
don't even know her name

he gives five dollars
has never given
dustier men and women
with rock eyes more than one

he pulls off
knows why
I am quiet

Auntie

You will die forgetting you once loved me.
Nose so close to my face now, palms

on my checks, trying to feel something
neither eyes nor memory can see.

Dying in a space that holds nothing,
but I guess that is all the better for you

not to know what you are losing.
All the people you have loved and unloved.

Best not to know your love for me turned
to hate once my calves and ass sprouted out

too much of you. Remember you said,
I had my day. It is your turn, but your day

will end. We were sitting on the piano stool.
Your green eyes greener. Your mind,

generations mad. Your strands gray.
Still swinging past your waist.

You believed the verse that says *hair is a woman's*
glory. Hair was everything. All you needed for Uncle

to take care of you. For the city to smile at you
through its windows. The light eyes, light skin,

long hair lies revealed when Uncle left for the brown-
eyed, dark skinned goddess with short hair. You caught

him cooing in her ear then held the barrel of the gun
in your mouth. I had no kind words for you,

till I discovered the power of cold metal against
the skin. It makes people come running to the one

who cries wolf. And like the townspeople,
the third time, Uncle thought you were bluffing.

Luckily, there were no bullets to swallow.
Auntie, I have had my day. The predicted

time has come. You can stop hating me now.
I know what it is like to lose everything

the world tells you matters. To coo
and be cooed to. Then disqualified

from the ranking. To tap metal against teeth,
inhale the barrel, massage it with my tongue.

Oomph

twists of lust, oiled gifts
to some graffiti, others rebellion,
but locks are the turf
where I land face first in soil
the strands, blades
the scalp, earth
the mane, hallucination,
each lock   a spirit   spinning
kaleidoscopic limb
twined around my waist.

I can't unravel myself
this time. He kisses
down sepia brown spine.
Knows where to turn. Skin
forsakes me again.

I might have to
go through this flame. Tonight,
I have this tickle,
this itch—intense hunger,

death of light.

After Our Pit Died on the Porch in My Husband's Arms

My husband sawed apart the chaise
where Scarlet used to sleep.

Fought against wood
and blade. Sawed until his palm

turned red and numb.
Dissembled each piece

with hammer, chisel,
pliers. Didn't ask for help.

There was something different
about his grief. Downstairs

every piece of furniture missing
backs or limbs. I wondered

if he would grieve
as deeply for me,

but didn't ask. That night
we dined at half a table,

and I licked everywhere
crumbs had fallen.

Rollerblader

Every morning, I watch the stranger with locks rollerblade
by my step.

I sit with one leg snaked over the other in a floral dress,
wearing ten billion colors

to compete with sunrise. My body, hidden and revealed
by moving shadows,

hopes to give him something in return for the gift he gives
me every dawn.

I perch on concrete in so many hues of brown overheated,
watching him dance

in white linen sweatpants and bare chest with birth
and death in his movements.

Citron, figs, and papaya on his tongue. He rattles and pumps.
My organs shift and swing

toward the sun, a black orchid, singing.

Bishop and His Assistant's Last
Rendezvous in the Church Basement

I'm not sure why Denise wanted to challenge her self-
righteousness. Kiss the guarded body beneath his robe.

Cosset his inhibited unholiness. Engage in a weekend
ritual of bone cracking tenderly against bone. But I saw

their last tryst on a Sunday. They were in his private quarters.
The headboard slammed against the concrete wall.

The First Lady was cooking for the Women's Ministry
in the kitchen on the floor above the rocking earth.

The mirror fell off its bureau. Bishop's heart stopped.
Denise crept out the basement door with images of their nude

bodies broken at angles in shards of glass. I picked up
the small ones with a gloved hand. Put them in a paper bag.

Swept up the rest with a broom and dustpan. Saved
the pieces I thought I could use to reconstruct his face.

Made a template. Smoothed and foiled the edges
of the glass. Soldered his features in place.

Drilled two holes in the pane. Suspended the stained
glass with rosary from a chain in my car window.

Comparing Stories at My Older Sister's Shower

You sit in a wicker chair
surrounded by pink roses

with a passel of girl cousins
around you, garlands of pastel.

One by one we let our stories
go, details of how Uncle

kissed, groped, or entered us.
We speak and these snakes

release into our homemade garden
of silk flowers.

Rays from the side window
warm your protruded belly

like it is sacred.
Like it is something

that will be protected.
It is your second pregnancy,

your husband's child.
The first was Uncle's.

Some would argue
it should have been

protected, too.
Would call you monster

for the choice you made.
Still, it wasn't easy.

I held your hand.
Cried with you.

But today,
we make a hat

with a plate
and satin bows.

Tie it loosely
beneath your chin.

Poem after Receiving My DNA Test Results

I've delivered sun streams and moon streams,
Siamese green swans in navy blue cages,

tangled seaweed, goblin shark skin,
tree stumps and tree trunks,

diamonds and dung, root fruit,
the Congo, Benin, Ireland and Italy,

buttocks and breasts, silk handmade
quilts, cotton, tobacco, sugar and shit,

sickled-celled slave holds, polluted
ocean dump, vines and ropes,

maples and oaks, virtue and vultures,
human wine and flesh-chunked

soil, mantle and crust, four billion
years of spine bone, and grime.

To the Women in the Family Who Wrote Before Me

They rise from the folds
of my knuckles, their miniature
arms anchoring pencil to page.

Limpid legs wrap
around the wood.
They are kids hugging
tree limbs, afraid to fall.

Wild with story, in need
of help, they press my fingers
like heavy feet on stiff pedals

and when I shake them off,
they return like boomerangs.
Trapeze artists who swing
from pinky to thumb.

Nibble on my hangnails.
Tickle my palms. Untwist
the seam of my sleeve.
Drum in time
to the pulse of my wrist.

They will not leave.
I cannot resist. Loud birds

these women—loud birds
with words for wings.

Afraid to Open This Letter from Inmate 17650-328

1.

Cliff's inmate number is on the left
corner of the envelope. It reminds me

of my visit to East Jersey State Prison,
a monstrous dome over a decrepit edifice.

Red brick. Appendages jutting from its sides.
A pointed roof at the end of each limb.

An enclosed yard crowned with spiked Slinkys.
The most ominous place I had ever been.

Everyone in my family had refused to see Cliff.
He had murdered his brother. I felt compelled to go.

2.

Five years prior, my father had died.
Prayer wasn't enough

to keep him alive. I found him on the floor.
Head in waste basket. Pants down.

Needle dangling from groin.
My mind had folded in on itself,

the indelible image incubating
in its creases. It had motivated me

to see Cliff. Motivated me to try
to find words to stop him from using.

3.

After I was frisked, fifty of us were jammed
into a small area with three walls. Battleship gray.

No ceiling. A fourth, a steel door, thundered down.
Guards, pacing the perimeter wall, told us

to tighten up. We got as close as we could,
nothing but fabric and sweat between strangers.

One tattooed face glared up at the guards
and cussed into the sky with passion and bass.

I caught one officer's eye, hoping he would notice
me in a mass of tight clothes, bamboo hoops,

and a thousand bracelets, but he knew
I had more in common with the other visitors

than I wanted to admit. He stared down
at me. Bellowed more commands.

I pulled on my pearls. Turned my diamond
ring around. Housed it in my palm,

so I would seem less pretentious.
Folded my arms across my body.

4.

Cliff was the cousin who took
me to his clubhouse, an abandoned

duplex that smelled like soot and urine.
We climbed broken steps.

Kicked through soiled rags,
one tan work boot without strings,

an eyeless Baby Alive Doll
like the one I had at home,

but mine was brown.
Still had its eyes.

I tripped around in jelly sandals,
yellow shorts, and a tie dye halter,

following Cliff and his friends.
I didn't think of heat,

rodents, or rusty nails.
When the cops came, Cliff held

his arms up and helped me escape
from the second floor window

onto a dirty mattress. Rode me home
on the handlebars of a stolen bike.

5.

Cliff and I are from Stanley Homes Village.
I moved to the suburbs when I was ten.

My mother sometimes left
me at Cliff's house.

I remember burying my face in the carpet
and covering my ears so I couldn't hear

my aunt strangle Cliff in his bedroom.
I never got used to that sound.

Out of all my auditory memories, it is the most
poignant, the sound of a dry drowning.

My mother stopped leaving me there,
and whenever I ran into Cliff, I could tell

he was becoming someone else.
Alcohol, pot, heroin. No sign of the boy

with wide eyes and straight As.
I didn't know the man I was visiting

in a maximum-security prison with a 30 year
sentence. When he walked into the courtyard,

bright orange and strong, I hugged the little boy
who had once held his arms out for me

just in case I had missed the mattress
when I jumped. The problem is I am now

watching everyone jump, but there are too many
windows. Not enough arms on the ground.

And although I know I was not responsible
for my father's life, and I am not responsible

for Cliff's life or the lives of everyone I am
connected to, I don't know how to love

without exhausting myself. I keep running from
window to window punishing myself every time

I miss. That's why I am afraid to open this letter.
I know I will do whatever it requires.

I will not write about you anymore

I've decided not to write
about how you were
and were not there.
How you cared,
but did not care.

I refuse to write
about how you
were a was
and a was not,
a sometimes,
an if, and a maybe

and a never
not ever father
who always is
but is not
a part of me.

Quietus

Brown flesh pours on grass, nourishing soil
for the goldenrod to resurrect in fall.

Bodily eruptions make life's faint worries
dissolve to the ground. Memories hoard

lust in separate mounds as sin's disfigured
shadow twists in torment beneath the crust.

Coarse hair coils between green blades,
then mashes into wet earth. Warm blood shades

white stones and quivering muscles lose themselves
in the rhythm of bones crackling to ash.

I am nothing. I
no longer can be found.

Today My Cousin Brenda Would Have Been Fifty

The woman we called *Morning* limped
down Ellington Street, asking for a dollar.

Everyone knew it was just a matter of time.
Government wasn't an enabler. No Narcan

to resurrect zombies. Folks dropped,
leaving brown puddles. Heroin ate people.

Every day a little thinner, disappearing
into clothes like ghosts. Till they were ghosts

on Ellington forever, their nothingness enough
to change moods of stray cats and dogs.

Morning would be no different. Last time
I saw her, she swallowed her teeth

before she opened her mouth to speak,
You remember me?

Did she mean from yesterday?
I searched her eyes, tried to look inside her.

We used to eat crayons together. I saw something
familiar. Delightful. Plates full of crayons.

Her sitting in a yellow romper.
Legs, hardwood floor-brown.

Two front teeth missing.
Mouth full of colored wax, laughing.

My Thoughts After My Mother Read Dana's Obituary

I am making too much
of this body that shares a space
with so many other
living and unloving things.

I have invested in a world
that will never love me
or the children I birthed
from my brown stitched womb.

I have depended too much
on my mind
that will eventually soften,
roll over and cry

trying to remember
things that don't matter
like the name of the little boy's
sister who lived next door,

Dana, two syllables with nothing
else to offer, not even a game
of checkers, jacks or Double
Dutch between us.

We could have been kinder
to one another.
Our skin tones were more
of a separation

than the chains
that divided the patch
of dirt between
our homes.

Dana was at the top
of *Black Bernice's* group
because Dana was the lightest
of the dark girls.

I was at the bottom
of *White Girl Cheryl's* group
because I was the brownest
of the light girls.

None of us were white,
but we had mastered the habit
of ranking, titled our chins up
to heaven, reached an arm

behind our own backs,
yanked a few strands
so hard we felt pain
at the root of our scalps

that opened our mouths
like ventriloquists'
dolls and swore
we were part Indian.

You remember her?
My mother asked, handing me
the newspaper.
She was the little dark girl next door.

Cute, though.

The Young Man in Barnes & Noble
Who Resembled My Son

I'm hungry.
Do you have a dollar?
I'm homeless right now.

"Right now" as if
I ain't always going to be
like this. Like if
you give me a dollar,
so I can eat, I can make it
through this night.

"I'm homeless right now" like
I wasn't supposed to be. Like this
won't always be my story.

I began to walk away,
but he looked like my son.
I can't lose this man.
I can't lose my son.

I walked him over to the cafe.
He got a plain bagel,
ham and cheese sandwich,
vanilla wafer, and Pepsi.

I was sure he wouldn't eat.
Sure he would order and wait
till I went out the front door
with an arm full of books,
and begged for more

dollars till he got enough
to get high in some corner
for the last time—his death,
a dollar from my pocket,

but I walked by the cafe
window on the way to my car.
Saw his hood and hair,
mouth pounding hard.

The Undertow

I keep going back in the ocean
to throw another child up on the jetty
and I can't swim, but I can't stop myself.
Everything I do is in response
to my father's death.

Grief and guilt are my buoyancy.

In 1991, he died of a heroin overdose
in an America that didn't
care about him.
I am angry.
I stay angry
even when I am laughing.

My dad came to me for prayer.
Admitted to slipping back.
Tugged my hand toward the floor.
We kneeled like children
in a prayer book.
Elbows on the cushion
of a blue sofa.

He thought my faith
had power. Thought my
God had answers. So, after his death,
I set out to prove that we
are not powerless.

I parented my children under
the weight of this grief.
Taught kids to read.
Wrote until my vision blurred.

Danced like I was trying
to get rid of something.

I am tired. I stay tired.
But not one day will go by
without me trying
to swim in an ocean that has tried
to drown me many times.

The first time, I was five.
My father was getting high
under the boards.
I strolled off in a red bikini, with a teal
pail full of seashells and sand.
I walked out too far.
Waves twisted me like seaweed.
The ocean was ready
to receive me like coral.

A lifeguard reached his hand down,
yanked me up by my braids,
and flipped me into a boat
with such force he bruised my back.
It is one of the greatest acts of love
I have ever known.

He did not love me,
but I think he loved
life, and maybe he loved
children or humanity.
It didn't matter
that I was brown.
That is how I want

America to love me.
That is how I wanted
America to love my father.

Whenever I get angry at white
America, I think of that lifeguard,
his pink lips over mine,
breathing breath into my lungs,
pale hands compressing
my chest. My ribs cracking
till I spit out an African
knifefish flapping without fins.

Now every day I grab
a brown child,
I realize we are both afraid
of the same water,
but I must pretend
I know what I am doing,
and sometimes after a long day
of throwing child after child
up on the jetty,

I want to stop moving.
Let the ocean have me

with one hand up.
Eyes wide open.

After Watching a Wren Sing on the Windowsill

I sing Teena Marie's "Out on a Limb"
to my husband in front
of our bay window.

I balance fishnet thighs
and swollen feet in red
stilettoes and he kisses

my body, the moles
on my neck and face. Our shadows
streak the nightlight-lit walls,

and although I do not understand
his pleasure, I know a woman's flesh
does not lose value over time.

So when his lips move across me,
when he speaks to the soft spots like
they have feelings, like they still carry

some miracle we've conceived,
I know I am holy.
Both in what has been lost

and what has been sustained.
Decades I have been out on this pane
and if I fly away

I want him to hear me singing,
chest out, beak agape.